D1028137

merritt k

TOTAL MOOD KILLER

Niina Pollari

ISBN 978-0-9970444-6-1

Cover and book design by SamDakota.

Printed in the United States of America.

For more information, visit www.tigerbeepress.com.

Total Mood Killer

merritt k

and

Niina Pollari

Table of Contents

merritt k

Table of Contents

Niina Pollari

merritt k

FAMILIAR

my problem is in the long term memory
i always forget what pain
or what no pain is

my brain is a baby cat
and the way things are right now
is the way they are always going to be
forever and ever

so we are leaving a wake of disasters

and i scold her but
she is just a baby cat
and doesn't know any better

a familiar could be a connection
to the devil or yourself

if you cast a line into the depths
and heave
you could drag up anything

so i carry her around and whisper:

that's *where you threw up from eating too fast*

your claws are getting bigger and sharper

let's *be careful*

EVERY MASCARA IS EXACTLY THE SAME

when in san francisco you took me
to the big cosmetics store
i was amazed at all the makeups

i wondered how many makeups
it would take for you to like me

five million
three hundred and
eighteen thousand
and eight

you see
i am a very funny girl

i am turning all the numbers upside down

i am talking to myself

THE SUMMER I LISTENED EXCLUSIVELY TO RUN THE JEWELS AND WALKED AROUND IN THE SHORTEST SHORTS I COULD FIND

i needed to feel untouchable
because when the portuguese-canadian
exuberance for football wins brought
mobile cop headquarters to st. clair and
lansdowne i had to have something
to help me sleep through the horns and
keep old men's hands at bay

i wanted to feel bigger, so
i wore my $30 tube of lipstick even
in the house and mentally inflated the rent money
trickling in from johns haggard in windsor
motels at two am until it seemed
like an exit strategy

it isn't until fall comes and the barricades
get packed away that you realize
there isn't an outside
some of us just take longer
to get there than others

LOVE TAP

brad pitt voice: i want you to hit me
as soft as you can

to feel your fists like
little chickadees alighting
on the goosebumped
surface of my skin

we could build tiny nests
in the cracks left by an overactive
history of geological activity

or whatever

a kid named hugh twisted my arm
until it popped and left me bleeding
in a gas station restroom

too proud to say uncle
or any other authority figure

A MILLION BILLION SCALES FALL AWAY

think of all the space you could fill
with the ways in which you're not enough

like a jellybean counting contest
except the jar is full of snakes

except that's rude to snakes

someone told me that in the original jungle book
kaa the snake was helpful
but they had to change it for the movie

because they didn't think anyone would believe
in the idea of a helpful python

now: think about turning the jar upside down

think about letting the snakes go free
in the middle of your junior high gymnasium

CLIFFHANGER

she said there's no such thing
as gender but somebody
still has to be the man one

all of the ads on casual encounters
couldn't convince me
that deep down everyone
doesn't want to be cradled

i will not put you
back in the loving
safety of the womb
or hold your hand
as you cross a comically
treacherous bridge
over troubled waters

i am busy clutching a
flimsy branch and
losing shoes to show that
this is serious

HEIST FILM

now picture me pursing my lips and practicing
sexy looks in the mirror
wearing polka dot panties
and a black balaclava

the caption reads:
on my way to steal your man

sorry to reinscribe heteronormativity
but it's the weekend

in middle school i was too chicken
so i stood watch to impress sporty girls
while they filled their pockets

the caption reads:
i am shoplifting everything i can

PERMANENT THURSDAY

every collar i've ever worn
has given me a rash

this is not a metaphor
which is another kind
of accessory

i'm starting to think you believe
there's virtue in being misunderstood

what i believe
is that it's gauche to give too much away

you keep your hand on the valve
and dispense only what is necessary

and you continue to resist the urge
to wrap your hand around the faucet
and spray everyone in the room

BACHELOR

a patina of dusty grease
has settled
over every surface
in the kitchen

and i guess what
it comes down to
is that i wish
i wasn't afraid

OVERABUNDANCE

sext: this
is a terrible idea
but the engine is
already running

in my head an abundance
of reasons to be cautious
repeated on an
accelerating loop

how long
until the whole mess
is thrown clear?

a car pulling out of a skid
sails into a highway median
in the snow
at night

QUEEN

post-sesh heavy tipping at tim hortons
like a slutty robin hood
tied up little fox boy planting
seeds of desire in everybody's heads

wanted sign: the fool, invasive species
object acting as aggressor by virtue only
of strutting in and sucking up
all of the air, sunlight, and attention

growing plump and wet
and withering with a glance

WHY IT WORKS

here's a secondhand story:
if i can believe
in you then you
can believe in me

and this is why it works, because
there's an elegant symmetry to it

two ships in the night
at odds with intended
purpose and each other
missing the pass and making
beautiful fireworks

TERRITORY

i eat an entire box of fruit
candy on the train home and pull
my bag up to my chest in
a tiny gesture of reduction

and you say i am taking
up too much space

and i suck in all the air and blow out my cheeks
and expand
and expand

until you realize that every
line you draw between us is
brittle and cracks like lollipops
when i am tired of waiting

GIRL ON THE SIDE

knowing you makes me want to be someone else
but in a good way

like i could
shave my hair or move apartments
and start fresh

new books and
clothes and affectations

meanwhile i sleep in your bed
while you spend the night at your girlfriend's

idea: an escort service but just
for someone to come over and let me sleep
in the crook of their arm
while they tell me that i'm good

an escort service for
girls who love to talk big
about being the fun one

swooping into town
with reservations for dinner
plans for exciting sex and infinite
emotional capacity

an escort service for
girls on the side
to keep us warm
while we lay in someone else's bed

entertaining fantasies of who
we might be if we lived here
and were home by now

FAULT LINE

suppose they could place your body
in a massive vice
and crush down your grace
jones shoulders into something narrow and correct

would you still feel after all that
like you were carrying everything

would you be able to stretch out tall
or would that feeling find a new home

slithering down your vertiginous spine
embracing your abraded knees
haunting the hollows of your hips

or nestling in the soles of your calloused feet

suppose atlas didn't shrug
but shifted from time to time
unobtrusively conscious
of the cost of every moment

WITCHING HOUR

1.
you leaned out your edinburgh
window and smoked a joint, movie
star topless
in the moonlight
i gave you my entire
fist but you
wanted more

2.
a firm hand centred on solar
plexus outside community bookstore,
pressing you, hot little thing in
leather jacket and slayer t-shirt, into
brick wall while men try
to catch a glimpse
of what we have

3.
grinding hips in the green room
behind the projector screen
you told me 'you don't
have to be afraid
of your body,' and i
thought that was a really
nice thing to say

WHAT I MEANT WHEN I HANDED YOU THE KEY

i'm tired of giving
i want you to take
everything about me
and crumple it into a
heap beside
the hissing radiator

later we can
do the work of unfolding
together, smoothing out
new lines with sure hands

for now, inward pressure,
compression, and
the tense promise
of a spring

GAY HIGH SCHOOL AU

for m.l.

in another world we are sulky
teen boys making out
behind the bleachers

what we can't find
words for we say with our hands
and teeth

fumbling towards the
sinewy rightness
of each others' bodies

ORDINAL

i like the phrase *devil's*
threesome because it implies to me
the existence of a spiritual ranking
of threesomes

i looked into a mirror that said
meet the person most responsible
for your safety
and that felt like a lot
of pressure

ideally
i would like to be standing
between two large men
with safe hands and
the devil watching

ASKED ABOUT MY IDEAL RELATIONSHIP
TO MY BODY

your beauty is a rock that you carry
in your pocket

you can feel its weight and shape
and if you want
you can draw it out carefully
like a baby bird

you can duck behind some bushes
and hurl it through a window

LOVE SONG FOR PRECARIOUS TIMES

1.
if you're broke
or your harness is,
hold your cock in your fly
and keep your hands
on your lover's hips
while you fuck her
(don't think about
rent or groceries,
it'll ruin
your rhythm)

2.
capital wants
to sell you polished pleasure
and sometimes it's worth it
but remember:
if you have hands, or feet
or teeth
you can use those too

3.
when you arrive
at a date's beautiful apartment
don't let yourself think
about what it would be like
to live there

4.
showering together
saves water
press your bodies together
to make the soap
go further

5.
buy expensive cocktails
sometimes and jump
into cabs together afterwards
don't think about the word
debt on the drive home: total
mood killer

6.
personal space
is important
but two people
sleep warmer than one
and three sleep
even warmer

7.
borders will keep you apart
when you get to talk
over cell signals
and fibre optics,
give her everything
join your love and fury
in holy, hungry matrimony

8.
when she comes trembling
and gasping, hold her and
whisper, *baby, you came hard enough*
to bring down capitalism

9.
pillow talk for the precarious:

i'm tougher
than the terms
of your loan repayments

your tits make me forget
all about
my overdraft fees

you don't owe me
anything

Niina Pollari

GOLDEN AGE

Golden Age of bringing your phone into the bathroom with
    you

I saw a commercial
For Opioid Induced Constipation
In it a sad woman slowly painted a snail

Golden Age of Opioid Induced Constipation
Golden Age of going to the bathroom as your alone time

I'm in the bathroom at work
Hiding out in one of the stalls
Other people can see my feet
It's a bathroom shared by the whole floor

Golden Age of going into the bathroom to cry

I look at the shoes of the people coming in
To see if I recognize them as my colleagues
And hope they do not get in the stall next to mine

Golden Age of not wanting to admit you still cry at work

Golden Age of checking your makeup on your phone
    before you exit the stall

This poem began in the bathroom
I walked into a stall
It's not a joke

I can't hover
I'm too tired
In my brain
Or I'm just
I don't know

My holey underwear loop around my calves
I'm careful to not let them touch the toilet

My string of eggs is coiled like a necklace
Around the blinding negative space
That lives inside me

Because of this deeply poetic description
Of some mostly invisible sex organs
I happen to own by circumstance

Nobody questions what bathroom I go into
When I need to pee or cry
Or check Twitter

Golden Age of being in the bathroom
Gloriously alone for once
I'm just standing here
Washing my hands

Staring past the mirror
At something, I don't know what

WHY CAN'T WE SEE THAT WE'RE LIVING IN A GOLDEN AGE

Asks some writer

According to him evidence shows

"Parts of the world are falling to pieces but fewer parts than before"

And the things you tend to notice are the bad things

Golden Age of sad hyperrealistic animations
That mimic the effects of depression
That I watch on my phone
Mostly at home

Golden Age of shows where guys milk a poison snake for its
    venom
It's weirdly macho and sexual
The venom is an insane green
I watch it on my phone

Golden Age of videos about animal attacks
There's something called "Untamed and Uncut"
That sounds like a porn

I think about how voyeuristic it is
That I can watch a shaky cellphone video of a cheetah
    climbing into a person's car
The graceful cheetah slithers in through the open window
    like a contortionist

Golden Age of taking something without permission

Do I have a right to watch it
If I don't pay for it

How can I pay
If I didn't ask for it

Does the person die
That's the cliffhanger
The animal almost always does

Just a friendly heads-up that you're getting close to using X GB
of data this cycle

Mobile data is throttled in the Golden Age
And devices become obsolete in two years

I have the phones from the last six years of my life
Stuffed inside various drawers in my house
They are meaningful to me
Like cooled friendships

I want to break up with them
Make them into art exhibits
Or throw them into the water
In a cinematic gesture
Like a protagonist

But for the environmental and nostalgia impact

Golden Age of nostalgic attachment
Golden Age of contaminated drinking water
Golden Age of conferences to address water governance
Golden Age of toxic e-waste dumps built and maintained in
    Ghana

The phone is your friend
And also contains poison
Which the kids at the dump have to pick through

Golden Age of toxic relationships

Or a friend you used to be incredibly close with
Who goes silent because you got a new friend
But keeps on living near you

Listen, I would miss my phones

REDDIT

Golden Age of porn
Golden Age of memes
Golden Age of television
Golden Age of eating ass
Golden Age of grotesque
Golden Age of federal government
Golden Age of nanotech and biotech research
Golden Age of superhero movies and online shows
Golden Age of high-alcohol IPAs and other craft beers
Golden Age of increasingly powerful and inexpensive
    computers
Golden Age of stupid whores being famous for being stupid
    whores

Pat yourself on the back
In the Golden Age you're doing everything you can
You're paying for new trees to be planted
When you use fossil fuels
To go on your tours

Keep a tally
Count your impact
Send the results to your Google Drive

It is nice to have a Drive

I count the words of progress
I made on this novel I've been working on
I like to see progress

Quantified work in the Golden Age
How much did you get done today
"You've written 5,738 words this month"

I am using a thing that backs up my drafts weekly
Some weeks my drive fills up with unchanged copies
Seeing the copies marked with their dates gives me
    personal guilt
Which motivates me
To work

Yesterday a young man talked to me about meditation apps
He said "I like to know how long it's been"

On my browser I have an extension that counts my age up
    to nine decimal points

Late in my office with a whiskey
My age increases as I nod at my screen

Golden Age of self-awareness

Granular time moves from a sugar bowl into an hourglass

If you are pregnant
You should secure your baby's gmail
While it's still a fetus
And time is still

On your side

There are so many things available for fetuses in the Golden
    Age
There are insertable vaginal speakers
That play music for them
To overcome barriers

Q: What barriers
A: The barrier of the body

Golden Age of new technology that overcomes barriers

In the Golden Age I am an early adopter of everything just
    in case

Do you worry about the future of your body
As it goes through its mystical processing

Do you worry that your impulses
For betterment and destruction
Are contradictory ones
Yeah

I poke two fingers into face cream
Hold them up like the hand of Christ
In icons or priests in benediction

Dab them under my eyes
And then scowl at myself in the mirror
My face is one of my assets and it's definitely starting to go

Golden Age of feeling like the whole of you is worth very
    little

I should eat less so I won't have a gut in these Instagrams

AUTOFILL

Golden Age is set up to be very homelike and has a very
relaxing atmosphere

Golden Age is a mythical time period held to be the ideal
state of humanity

Golden Age is an optimistic song on a mostly pessimistic
album

Golden Age is the period when a specified art is at its peak

Golden Age is now. We're hardwired not to believe this

Golden Age is an offline turn-based strategy game

Golden Age is a myth at best or a failure

Golden Age is subversive and it's fun

Golden Age is an often imaginary past time of peace,
prosperity, and happiness

In the Golden Age I go to sleep worried
And then have anxiety dreams

In them
I go to work
Update my LinkedIn
Get called unambitious
For not desiring a management track
Then find a Klonopin on the floor and take it

Like a pigeon
Busting open a foam clamshell
Of street cart rice and chicken bones
And eating it and throwing it around
Ecstatically

I have only so much space in my mind
When I am in public
To hold respect

For myself

Golden Age of gaslighting
Golden Age of income disparity
Golden Age of no vacation policy
Golden Age of nonmonetary incentives
Golden Age of Medium posts full of rhetoric

*I have decided to move on from Company X and to explore
other options*

I have it good, I know
I'm in a liberal bubble

I get paid like almost enough
I've never had to use sick days to care for my children

For example

But IDK

MEDIUM POST

Golden Age of paid content
Golden Age of content creators

Golden Age of luxury pool toys
Golden Age of real fear

Golden Age of dirty talk
And silence

Golden Age
Of something

It's coming

If I were to speak
In a first-person-as-collective voice
Well then I could say

I go online first thing in the morning
Or Twitter or Facebook or any app made for connecting
Like a plant putting out feelers

I am not alone
I am not alone

The feeling of urgency
A storm drain backing up
There are so many physical ways
To feel lonely

Not feeling rested
Unsettled stomach
Addictive behavior
Motivated by desolation
Physically dreaming too much
I am the first person to ever do this

It doesn't go away

The plant in me
Has a huge taproot
And it demands so much water

It will grow as deep as it needs to grow
To find it

A wildfire mushrooms in California

A hurricane trims the bangs of the Florida coast
Twenty inches of rain drop on Louisiana
Like the ice bucket challenge

We have to find a fire boyfriend
A hurricane boyfriend
I feel it so for real

Golden Age of viral proposal videos
Practice your surprise face
Know your best angles
Become a viral video
Then add virality
To your resume

Even passing the baton
Of your loneliness to the next person
Is an accomplishment
Best made in public

I have to tell you something
When I got married this year
I shared a ring pic on my social

I don't know that this is in the "we" voice anymore

Golden Age of

. . .

Of controlling your brand

Golden Age of one thing becoming you in your entirety

Like when the one known thing about you is viral

Golden Age of the public spectacle

School X rape accuser brings mattress to graduation, defies administration

Golden Age of people who aren't doing anything wrong

Did good grades, good home get student profiled as rapist?

Golden Age of dropping out due to mental illness

Golden Age of having to crowdfund medical expenses

Pre-dawn on my couch
I open Craigslist

The ads in gentrifying neighborhoods
Mention coffee shops and optimistic travel times to
     Manhattan

They describe the neighborhoods as "up-and-coming"
As if they've been uninhabited all this time
And are just being discovered

Golden Age of justifying your move with your own sad
     financial state

In the Golden Age of landlords who fill buildings
In historically black neighborhoods
Full of white girls in cardigans
Finding a rental has always been fast for me

I told myself it was because of my good credit
Golden Age of believing that debt is an advantage

Get up
Put on your jacket
Complain about the commute

Finally say hi to the neighbor two buildings down from you
After passing him every day for months

I distrust my own memories

I used to use the ATM that dispenses $10 bills
To buy a bodega sandwich and a beer
And then stay up all night
Out of loneliness

Even this is tinged with nostalgia

Golden Age of buying loosies at dawn like it's a novelty
Golden Age of ordering food delivery to your home during
    a snowstorm
Golden Age of taking an Uber when the train is shut down
    because of a cop killing
Golden Age of your landlord asking that you not disclose
    your rent to the newer tenants

In the Golden Age people combine lives out of economic
    convenience
The times when I did it always ended badly

Even if I lived small and contained
Even if I secured the bathroom door
And propped my computer on the toilet
To watch episodes of Intervention from the tub

Still I only found
Myself enervated

If I went out
I was unable to return
And turn the key in the lock

I just slumped on the doormat
Until somebody let me in

Golden Age of being bloodless with anger all the time
Golden Age of the rat's ass that you give
Even when you keep on giving it

When the heart
Sinks low in the body

Its long throat full of ashes
And lays down like a dog

Some time before I got married I insisted on living alone
In my own apartment separate from my partner's
    apartment

As proof of something
Like independence

Maybe to show that I had self-respect
Maybe as a gesture of love

A fantasy of autonomy

That I wasn't economically reliant
That my choosing someone was a real choice
That lack of money wasn't going to make me repulsive
That I was never again going to pack up someone's things

While the next tenants to share the shitbox
I was leaving behind —

Its matchstick contents dumped illegally inside
Multiple municipal trash cans along the avenue —

Waited in a U-Haul parked across the street
Smoking and glaring at me

Or something

Golden Age of righteous anger
Is that what you call this
Little rising bile

I joined this poem for selfish reasons
I feel grateful but also
Not at all

Everybody keeps trying to explain
Why things are going wrong

A huge mouth
With a polemical answer
Trailing out of it like lyrics to a song poised to be popular

If you watch any conversation for more than two minutes
It will always return to money
Tacitly or not

I ride a train to a plane to a car to visit family
And then I lie around draining my battery

I am lying on a quilt looking at my phone in the Golden Age
I retire to the bedroom even though nobody retires
In the Golden Age
Nobody has savings

My heart is a hairy caterpillar
That won't molt unless it gets paid

In the old neighborhood where I paid
Less money than my building's other inhabitants
But more than the original black residents of the
    neighborhood

The cops erected towers
And flooded the housing projects with 1250-watt lights all
    night
I read something about the glare of these lights

That they're so bright they're no longer allowed to be
    pointed at detainees at Guantanamo

And all night as people went about their night business
The cops stood around the light towers staring
Or quietly talking to each other

Golden Age of comprehensive plans to retrain the police
    force

Every time I walked past I didn't look them in the eyes
Or I muttered "fuck the police" under my breath as if it was
    something

Fully knowing they didn't give a shit about me
In my cardigan

The Golden Age describes an era of "superiority"

A time specific in a culture when something is going really
    well

Like nationalism or voter suppression or police brutality or
    PTSD

History has always gone really well for some participants

And some Golden Ages stagger over each other

And are even more Golden than other Ages

Still there is a temporality to the phrase

That is both difficult to stomach

And anticipatory

I am in the kitchen
Doing some dishes

This poem began in a bathroom and ends in a kitchen
Does the domesticity of that feel apolitical
I'm not really asking

Golden Age of small acts

In an apartment in another neighborhood
The square shoulders of a tall new condo
Block my view of the Empire State Building

This building is old
The floor slants

I'm holding a crumbling smiley-face sponge
And noodling around with this poem

Some of the words of which
Have spun around in me for years
Like sink water with food debris in it

Getting caught
Like garbage in the mesh
Strainer of the sink

The pieces build up
Until the water no longer drains
And you need to dig them out with your fingers

Still you need to do something with them

Golden Age of knowing you are responsible

Yes I know what the next step is

Acknowledgements

merritt k is a writer and podcaster. Her first book, *Videogames for Humans*, is an exploration of contemporary interactive fiction and was nominated for a Lambda Literary Award for Best LGBT Anthology. She hosts the podcasts Woodland Secrets and dadfeelings, and can be found on Twitter at @merrittk.

merritt k thanks Kay Gabriel for critical commentary and the following journals who first published versions of these poems:

The Collapsar: "Familiar"

SCUM Magazine: "Gay High School AU"

Heavy Feather Review: "What I Meant When I Handed You The Key"

Nat. Brut: "Asked About My Ideal Relationship To My Body"

Alien Mouth: "Ordinal"

Niina Pollari is the author of *Dead Horse* (Birds, LLC/Emily Books, 2015) and the translator of Tytti Heikkinen's *The Warmth of the Taxidermied Animal* (Action Books 2012). She tweets at @heartbarf.

Niina Pollari thanks Monica McClure and Allyson Paty for their comments on versions of her poem along the way.

TigerBee Press is an independent, Brooklyn-based publisher specializing in chapbooks and similarly potent limited run projects.

Previous titles include:

Prostitute Laundry

N.B.

Color Me Gray

3 Conversations

On Balance

Bad Drawings by Bad Women

www.tigerbeepress.com